12 DAYS WITH GOD

Devin Sherman

2016

Unless otherwise noted, all scripture quotations are from the New King James version of the Bible

12 Days With God

ISBN: 978-1-329-81660-2

Copyright© 2016 by

Devin Sherman

Syracuse NY 13206

Published by D&L Publishing NY

Printed in the United States of America

All rights reserved under International Copyright Law.

Contents and/or cover may not be reproduced in whole or in part in any form without the express written consent of the publisher

DEDICATIONS

This book is dedicated to my loving wife, Lisa and my little princess, Isabella. During this time in our lives you are the muse for my fight to live. You are my inspiration and I will live out the rest of my days showing you both how thankful I am to God for the two of you.

To my brother Colin and his wife, Diane. Thank you for your prayers and laughs during this time in our lives. You two are always on time. I love you both immensely.

To my parents, Jamal and Deborah Bogor. You are my prayer warriors and I am thankful to you for showing me the path to God. You never gave up on me, even when I wanted to give up on myself. May God reward you richly.

To Ernie, Eda, Ernie Quinones Jr., Glorisel Hernandez and Arminda Correa (Buelita). Thank you for opening up your home to me after my surgery. You are my family and I love you all as if I have known you all my life.

To my surgical team, Dr. Salvatore Caruana, Dr. Michael Kazim and Dr. Christine Rhode. God's hands worked miracles through yours during my 26 hours of surgery. You have no idea how grateful I am to you. You are all blessed and highly favored in the eyes of God for your expertise and excellent care of one of His children. Thank you.

To my Aunt Dr. Valerie Torrence. You lost the battle to cancer, but you gained eternal life with Christ. You have left an impression on me that will last a lifetime. You are one of the strongest women I know and I am in awe of your accomplishments. You are one of God's greatest creations.

To the amazing prayer team at Abundant Life Christian Center. God heard your prayers and He replied with complete and total healing. Pastor Carl and Pastor Jeanne....it is better than I could have imagined.

To my oncologist, Dr. Rahul Seth. You are one amazing doctor. I believe not only did I find a great doctor, but I also gained a friend.

DEVOTIONAL

I was born out of a womb into a world of sin

I had seizures as a child and slept in rooms with no heat

Since birth anger and I were best friends

I created a world that only I lived in

I have seen people die right in front of me

And hurt innocent people for money

I have walked amongst the dead

And smoked cigars with demons

Slept on dirt floors

And sold drugs to empty souls

Used fear as intimidation

Did good deeds only to escape death

Got drunk and fought in bars

Raced cars

Took drugs to calm my brain

Always smiled to hide the pain

But You God, You found me one night in a hotel room and decided that enough was enough. You allowed me to go into the depth of my own hell, so I would call on You to raise me up. I am a work in progress, but You have never given up on me. You have shown me what a Father with unconditional love is. You have shown me that I am forgiven and my past has made me who I am today. You have surrounded me with blessings and a new life. I will live out the rest of my life serving You.

INTRODUCTION

Hello and good day to all. My name is Devin Sherman. On May 26th 2014, while coming home from visiting family during the Memorial Day weekend, I discovered a bump on the right side of my face. After feeling some discomfort and arriving home from our four hour drive from New York City, I was compelled to visit my local urgent care. Upon my visit, the doctors drew blood and took a computerized axial tomography (CAT) scan of my head. After viewing the scan, they found a mass growing on the right orbital bone. It had done extensive damage to the right side of my face even though by looking at me I showed no signs. The only inclination outside of the mass on the scan, was that my right eye had also pushed out slightly. I was then sent to the local hospital for further tests and observation. After spending more than six hours in the hospital, I was met by two ear, nose and throat (ENT) specialist that informed me that they would like for me to come into their office later in the week for a follow-up. This was all on a Monday. I had scheduled an appointment for that following Wednesday. During my appointment, I was told that the doctors had no idea what was causing the mass or the deconstruction of my facial bone. The only way to be sure was with a biopsy.

THE BIOPSY

I was scheduled to have my biopsy the following Wednesday. When I arrived at the specialty clinic for an outpatient surgery, my wife by my side, a million upon a million thoughts were swimming around in my head. I tried to act as if this day was like any other normal day, but unfortunately it wasn't. My biopsy took less than two hours and I was headed home to rest (like that was going to happen) and wait for the results.

THE RESULTS

After about a week and a half I could no longer wait for the results. My wife and I called to see why the delay in the results, and why no one had reached out to us. I was informed that the mass growing inside of my face was indeed a malignant tumor. But they had no way of classifying what type it was nor how I got it, better yet, how to treat it. As you could imagine my entire life at that very moment stopped!!....Me....Cancer.......Cancer.....Me, this is not possible! I am a very strong, and athletic man. I don't do drugs. I don't drink "a lot." I have a cigar once in a blue moon. How could this be? Of course all I could do next was look over at my wife, who was trying extremely hard to hold back every emotion possible. See, we had just been married two years prior to the day May 26th. The day that I went to urgent care was also the day of my anniversary. It is also the day that set all of these events in motion.
 Also, we had a little girl just over a year before. I thought about what would I tell my two older children? How would everyone around me be affected by this? We continued to ask a barrage of questions to the doctor, who at this time had very little information to give us, other than--- I had cancer. He had informed me that they were sending the biopsy to a larger cancer center in New York City for a better analysis and description of the tumor.
 Just another thing I had to think about until we knew exactly what we were dealing with.

THE RESULTS OF THE RESULTS

After waiting an additional two weeks, I finally met with my oncologist who informed me that my cancer had a name. I had a high grade Sarcoma growing in my face. OK, now that we know…what do we do about it? The oncologist informed me that the cancer was treatable and curable. I had a strong immune system, and I was still young enough to fight this thing. The only issue was that my type of Sarcoma is so rare, that only four percent of all people in the country have or have had it. This is not how I wanted to be considered "special", or "unique". I was told that the next step would be radiation, followed by chemo then surgery, or surgery then chemo. Either way, all I could think about was thanking God that I could be cured. Second thought was, whatever needs to be done, "Let's do it".

A lot of people have that moment in their life when they feel as though they are all alone. When finding out that I had cancer, I felt the entire world zero in on me, as if I was the only person on the planet. I couldn't see anyone or even hear anyone. All I could do was stare at the doctor as I saw his lips moving, but I could not hear the words coming out. I felt this way again when I went to my oncologist and he informed me that even with surgery and chemo, losing my right eye was inevitable. Through all this I was not looking for this outcome. As I arose the next morning, after a night of anguish, I realized that the whole time since my diagnosis, I had been believing for complete and total healing through faith and the word of God. Yes I realized that my faith would be tested and sometimes what I might hear would scare me, but it's my faith that kept me at peace. My God said that He will never leave me nor forsake me, and through the blood of Jesus I am healed. I had to stand on this in order to keep my sanity.

12 DAYS WITH GOD

Dedication	pg. 3
Devotional	pg. 5
Introduction	pg. 7
The Biopsy	pg. 8
The Results	pg. 9
The Results of the Results	pg. 10
Surgery day	pg. 13
Recovery from first surgery	pg. 15
Unconditional love	pg. 17
Devotion	pg. 22
Reconstructive surgery	pg. 27
Faith	pg. 31
Release	pg. 36
Forgiveness	pg. 42
Words	pg. 46
Prayer	pg. 51
God's Word (the Bible)	pg. 54
Reflection (morning of release day)	pg. 57
Release day continued	pg. 59
Conclusion	pg. 61

SURGERY DAY

I was told to be at the hospital for admission at 6 a.m. It was going to be the longest stay I had ever had in a hospital. I wasn't alone by any means. I had a barrage of family with me for support. I was being admitted to have the orbital tumor in my right eye removed and then reconstructive surgery to put back in place what the cancer had destroyed. There was some uncertainty to this surgery because the doctors didn't know if my eye could be saved. We had prayed the week before and a prophecy from God, spoken through my pastor, would be that my surgery would be the best that any of the surgeons could expect and that they would in turn be amazed at the works of their own hands. So, even though I was nervous for surgery, God was with all of us during this time and His words have always been true. We all sat in the waiting room until the nurse came out and sent just me and my wife to the pre-op room to meet with the doctors and get me prepared in my gown and hospital socks. There was a slight change in my surgery procedure and we would be incorporating a neurosurgeon into the mix along with the three surgeons that were already scheduled. The reason for this was, that the best way to access a part of the tumor was by removing a small part of the skull right above my eye. I felt somewhat hesitant at the news of this new procedure, but just as soon as this doubt came, so did peace. I took with me the words that were spoken over me and the doctors. That nothing other than excellence was to be expected.

It was now time for me to go from the pre-operating room to the operating room. Along with a nurse, I was followed by my entourage of family. We got to a long corridor where only the nurse and I could go. I gave hugs and kisses to my wife and family. As I walked down this long hallway, I felt such a warmth and sense of calm come over me. My body went into a complete sense of relaxation and I turned to my family who was still watching me and said "don't be sad, God's got this", gave a quick wave and walked into the operating room. I was met by my complete surgical team that shook my hand as I was instructed by my anesthesiologist about what I could expect. Even though I could hear every word coming from her mouth, and I could see all my surrounding, I was not in the same place they were. Physically, yes I was laying on the table but spiritually my focus was on God.

RECOVERY FROM FIRST SURGERY

I don't remember much from my first night of recovery. I just remember being in a green post-op room with the nurse telling me how quickly I was recovering from my surgery. I wasn't there more than a half an hour before they moved me upstairs to my room, where I would be until my second surgery which was five days away. Once there, my wife came in with tears in her eyes and informed me that they were able to save my eye from being removed. My surgery's original time of completion was to be seven hours. I was in there for eleven hours. During the course of speaking with my wife and other family members, they proceeded to inform me of how the events took place during my operation. First, is that during the first few hours into the surgery, the eye surgeon came out and told the family that the tumor had breached the membrane that separates the orbital socket from the outside skin and muscle that makes up the outline of the face, so saving my eye was unlikely. Certain members felt that something was not right, this is not how the outcome was to be. Some of them prayed as others stood in agreement. Within a few hours, the same doctor came out and informed them that not only was he able to save my eye, but he was able to resect all the tumor, and that all the margins around the tumor were clean. We later found out that after the conversation that he had with my family, he too went back inside and felt that something was not right with the outcome and that there was more he could do to save my eye. He proceeded to clear away as much bone and fat tissue that could be frozen and sliced. The bone sections had to be sent out to pathology to wait for results but the fatty frozen sections could be tested in the operating room. The outcome was outstanding. The margins from the fatty tissue were clean, meaning all the cancer had been removed. After forty eight hours we were told the bone section margins shared the same outcome, again-clean. The overall diagnosis; I was cancer and tumor free!

UNCONDITIONAL LOVE

Unconditional love: meaning not subject to any conditions.

The morning of my third day, I was thinking of all the prayers that had gone up for me. I found myself praying to God and thanking Him for keeping His word when it came to the outcome of my surgery. It was at this time that I heard the words "I love you more than you know and you will start to see the unconditional love that I have for you" I was blown away by these words that truly came down from God himself. At that moment a warmth came over me, kind of like when someone hands you a blanket that just came out of the dryer. It was a warm and loving comfort that surrounded me from head to toe. I knew that God was speaking to me. At that point, I didn't have any doubt that this surgery would go any other way than the way my Father had already revealed to me along with a group of others. It was to be better than expected. Something else came over me as I basked in this ambience of divine and untouched love, and that is for me to love the same as God was loving me, without judgment, discrimination or reservation. God was showing me His love so I, in turn, would share my unconditional love the same way. It's a freedom that we have to look beyond someone's shortcomings, (for we all have them), and see the person that God has put on this earth and love them no matter what. Walking in divine love is hard and sometimes challenging, especially when you must continue to love those that hurt you. In the Bible it says to pray for your enemies, despite their transgressions against you. Anyone who comes against a child of God will have to deal with His wrath. By praying for them, you release them to God to be dealt with and it frees you from anything that will be brought against them. God does not want us to waiver from our love walk. His son Jesus had many who hated and despised Him, but He continually walked in love. This doesn't mean that you won't get mad or angry at someone, it just means that because of your love for them, you will love them enough to pray that God shows them the error of their ways. There will be consequences for someone coming against you as a child of God, but just like any father, God's discipline does not mean that there is a lack of love. If anything, it means that God loves us all enough to set us straight. Parents discipline their children not because they dislike them, but because they know that without discipline, the future for their children may become challenging and that by not using discipline, they are doing their children an injustice.

Another thought came over me that there was something that I had always struggled with and that struggle was with how I loved others. I always felt that love had to be proven by measures of saying "I love you", with the other party reciting it back as a confirmation. God brought my wife to my attention. He put this woman in my life to shower her with a love that for so long I never knew existed. I was now seeing her in a way that after being together for nearly six years and married for two, was just astounding. It didn't matter if she said she loved me on a daily basis or if I even said it to her. What mattered was that she was a gift from heaven and

God reminded me to love her as His son Jesus loved all of us enough to die for our sins. The same goes for family. God showed me that even if I don't agree with the lifestyles of my family or don't approve of all of their decisions that my love for them has to be unmovable. If God removed His love or questioned His love for us every time we did something He didn't approve of, we would be lost and even more completely helpless. It's because of God's love for us that we are able to go on living another day, despite our sinful and sometimes unjust ways. Even those who praise God daily and are devoted to serving Him, still are not worthy of His unconditional love. It's because of His love and mercy and graciousness for us that we are blessed to continue with our lives. So, I have a newfound love for all whom surround me. I want them to know, that I am always here to love and support them no matter what. I may not always agree with them, but that doesn't matter when it comes to unconditional love and the power that love possesses.

1 John 4:7-11

[7] Beloved, let us love one another: for love is of God; and every one that loveth is born of God, and knoweth God.

[8] He that loveth not knoweth not God; for God is love.

[9] In this was manifested the love of God toward us, because that God sent his only begotten Son into the world, that we might live through him.

[10] Herein is love, not that we loved God, but that he loved us, and sent his Son [to be] the propitiation for our sins.

[11] Beloved, if God so loved us, we ought also to love one another.

NOTES:

DEVOTION

Love, loyalty, or enthusiasm for a person, activity, or cause.

The morning of my fourth day in the hospital. I woke up and sat in my hospital chair staring out at the scenery of the George Washington Bridge. I began to pray and ask God to show me my heart and what I am missing. God then revealed to me that I had to become more devoted to Him. I had to stop using Him as a bartering tool as if to say "God if you get me out of my situation I promise to go to church or pray more". This is not the relationship that God wants with us. He wants us to be truly devoted and enthusiastic about serving Him. He does not want us to be ashamed to use His name when asked why we are so happy and blessed. We are quick to say that we know someone famous, but in reality there is no other name more famous than God. I found myself feeling ashamed that I would ask God for things and when He provided I would say "thanks God". I never showed my true appreciation or excitement that my Heavenly Father answered my prayers. Instead it was on to the next thing I could ask God for. All God wants from us is devotion, showing Him how much excitement we have for Him and His word.

Take a husband and wife for instance. You get married and at the altar you say your vows in front of friends and family announcing your love for one another. You proceed to say that you now devote your life to this person until death do you part. Devote, what a powerful word to use when you are speaking about how you will adore, be excited about, be faithful, loyal and committed to this other half of you for the rest of your life. So many people miss the mark on this and never truly understand what devoting yourself to one another is truly about. Yes, it sounds so romantic and so right to say, but are you ready to make this pledge of allegiance for the rest of your life? People get so hung up on saying things that they really either don't mean or don't understand the true magnitude of the words they speak.

Devoting your life to God is just that, Devotion. Committing your life to following God's law and being excited to do so. Praising Him shows your appreciation and praying to Him is an exercise of your faith and that you believe in His word. God is devoted to us even when we are not committed to Him. God will take care of our needs even when we are not deserving of anything. So many times I have prayed to God and He answered my prayer even though I was not worthy. God is true to His word and He said that He would never leave us nor forsake us, even if we are not worthy of what we seek from Him. The difference is, that what I was praying for and believing, was not even close to what God truly has for me, and what waits for me if I only seek Him, completely devote my life to Him, and shower Him with my praise and prayers.

I made a commitment to my wife when we got married to be a faithful and committed husband, to show true devotion to her and the family that we raise. I took that oath before her and God and was excited to show her how dedicated I am to her. I thank God for her. With that being said I have since my surgery, devoted my life to serving My God on an even greater scale than before. Even though I was not worthy of His healing and His love as I laid on the operating table for two surgeries with a total time of 26 hours, God still kept His word to me for complete and total healing from cancer. When I left that operating room and went into recovery, my wife and family were informed that what we had been praying for and believing in, (complete and total healing) was what we received. If I can devote my life to a woman whom I only knew for six years of my life and who I truly knew was sent to me by God, then there is nothing more I need to see or experience to devote my life to God, who has always kept me in His embrace even when I didn't deserve to be there.

Colossians 3:17 - And whatsoever ye do in word or deed, [do] all in the name of the Lord Jesus, giving thanks to God and the Father by him.

Matthew 22:37 - Jesus said unto him, Thou shalt love the Lord thy God with all thy heart, and with all thy soul, and with all thy mind.

Hebrews 11:6 - But without faith [it is] impossible to please [him]: for he that cometh to God must believe that he is, and [that] he is a rewarder of them that diligently seek him.

Proverbs 3:5-8

5 Trust in the LORD with all thine heart; and lean not unto thine own understanding.

6 In all thy ways acknowledge him, and he shall direct thy paths.

7 Be not wise in thine own eyes: fear the LORD, and depart from evil.

8 It shall be health to thy navel, and marrow to thy bones.

NOTES:

RECONSTRUCTIVE SURGERY

On the morning of day five, I woke up with a churning in the pit of my stomach. Although the first surgery went well with removing the tumor from my face, now came the time where they were putting me back together to look as much like I did before I came to the hospital. I woke up around five or so and spoke to my wife who was already in route to see me. My brother and his wife were not far behind. I had a brief moment to speak with God on this morning and all I could remember saying to Him was that it all was in His hands. He promised me divine healing and that is exactly what I trusting Him for. But still after going through an eleven hour surgery, just five days prior, I was feeling uneasy. I didn't know why, but all I could do was pray to God and ask that He remove this fear. Once my wife, in-laws, brother and sister-in-law showed up, my mind switched from worry to making them feel at ease by making them laugh and letting them know everything was going to be alright. This was God's way of relieving my anxiety. It was great to see all of these people who love me surrounding me in support. I remember joking with my brother and my wife about the intern that brought me down to pre-op. He was a small man and he had the task of taking my 230lb. frame and bed down to the prep room. Needless to say he had the worst time ever. He couldn't control the bed and we ended up hitting possibly every wall en route to the prep room. I wasn't hurt but I found this hysterical and this was another way for my mind to be diverted from my overthinking. I can truly say that God does have a sense of humor and He knows exactly what to do to get your mind in a better place. This was something He knew I would find comical. Once we got to the pre-op room, I was prepped and met all of my operating team that would be reconstructing my face to the best of their ability. Once that was done, I had to sign all the approvals for surgery, then off to the operating room. I was in the same room that I was in before and once again, as they laid me on the table, a sense of calm came over me. It's like God was laying me down to take a nap. I was no longer worried or even concerned. This was the way He wanted this to go and the outcome would be magnificent. My surgery was scheduled for eight hours, but I ended up being in for fifteen hours. I was later told that once my surgery was over, I immediately woke up and tried to walk off the table. I was unaware that they took part of my hip to rebuild my cheekbone and to give all the titanium that was put in my face, something to bond with. I ended up with facial titanium mesh, titanium plates and a bone graft from the iliac crest bone from my hip. Even though I couldn't see how amazing the operation was, I was glad that it was finally done. God truly held to His word that this operation would be better than expected. I was transferred from the operating room to the recovery room and stayed there for three days before being moved upstairs, where once again I got a view of the George Washington Bridge. I was visited from the anesthesiologists and he proceeded to ask me if I felt anything during the surgery. I replied that I didn't and asked him why. His answer was because I tried to get up right after surgery and they felt that I was awake at some point during the operation. I knew right then, that God woke me up to astound and show these doctors that they were operating on a man of God. All I could do was thank my Heavenly Father that I had come through this with Him overseeing everything. At the time it didn't matter what I looked like, I was alive and I was without cancer. I was eager for God to continue to spend the following days with me, showing me more of the life lessons that would make my walk with Him more profound and meaningful. He does what He says He is going to do and I cannot wait for more.

Isaiah Chapter 41:10-Fear thou not; for I [am] with thee: be not dismayed; for I [am] thy God: I will strengthen thee; yea, I will help thee; yea, I will uphold thee with the right hand of my righteousness

Deuteronomy 31:6: Be strong and of a good courage, fear not, nor be afraid of them: for the LORD thy God, he [it is] that doth go with thee; he will not fail thee, nor forsake thee.

Genesis 28:15: I am with you and will watch over you wherever you go, and I will bring you back to this land. I will not leave you until I have done what I have promised you.

NOTES:

FAITH

Complete trust or confidence in someone or something.

Faith...oh this is such a big word to be only five letters long. Faith, believing in someone or something without seeing the outcome or even knowing if it exists. God does exist and there is no greater way to show Him that you believe in His word than your practice of faith. On my sixth day in the hospital, this was the lesson that God had for me. Where did I stand when it came to my faith in God and all that He said would be done as long as I trusted in Him? I had to look deep to see where I was with this. I always believed in God, but even when God would say "Trust in Me", I would agree and then shortly thereafter, I would find a million and one ways to do it myself instead of waiting on God. I took on work that eventually lead to stressful situations, which lead to high blood pressure medicine, sleepless nights, and constant headaches. Why? Because I didn't put my trust and faith in God. I figured He gave me a problem solving brain and that's what I was to do, figure it out and fix it myself. I was even told by my Pastor to wait for God to bring in the work for my business and not go out and try to "make the ultimate deal" just to prove that I could make it happen. Then the ultimate test came in June, when I was diagnosed with a rare bone cancer called Osteosarcoma of a high grade. My world stopped and now came the true test of my belief in God and all the promises that He made to me. I remember wondering whether or not I brought this upon myself and why this was happening? Then

I remembered-as I was working on two major projects; stressing over a failed project; not eating (except for dinner), not exercising (which I love to do), and not resting. In the month of February I heard the word "STOP". I also remember hearing this same voice some two years prior, telling me to eat well, exercise and rest. I just ignored these signs and kept pushing on to the next thing hoping for a break. Why wasn't anything going smoothly, why was I continuing to fall into these stressful positions? Doesn't God know that I have bills, school tuitions, etcetera, etcetera, etcetera? Then I got my answer, "You didn't wait on me, said the Lord." God said that He would take care of all my needs as long as I waited and had faith in His word. I had to back down from trying to be in the lead and let my Heavenly Father lead me. I wanted to prove to my wife and kids that "I got this." In reality I was actually pushing farther away from what God had for me. I got myself so worked up, stressed and angry that things weren't working out, that my body finally said, "ENOUGH! You will no longer abuse me." My body was telling on me and I had to obey it. Now I had to listen to God, I couldn't get myself out of this one. I couldn't work my way out of cancer. I finally said to God, "I trust You with all that I am. Please heal me and make me whole." I finally decided to do what God had always wanted me to do; let Him guide and provide, turning everything over to Him so He can be glorified. All He wants to do is provide and watch us grow in Him and succeed on earth. This is how I should have been thinking from day one, but of course so many of us don't. I was part of that crowd. Completely trusting in God and His word, since I turned it all over to Him, has been the best thing that I could have done. God has proven to me that all I need to do is have faith in His word. His word is always true and He knows what's best for you even when you don't. Faith, such a magnificent word. It releases you from daily stressors by giving all your worries over to God and letting Him guide and provide for you. You have to also understand this; when you let your faith grow to new heights, opposition will come. Opposition is the test of your faith, the means by which you can stand on God's word and not be moved by what you see, but rather by what God has said He would do for you during that time. All those who believe in God and follow His word are destined for something great. The problem is when we get impatient, we try to accomplish our desires by doing things ahead of God's timing. In turn, we set ourselves back instead of moving forward. Having faith in God's timing and His promise to us will keep us at peace and when things come to hinder those promises that were made to us, we can stand on God's word because His promises are always true. We can never fully imagine what the Lord has planned for us, because our minds can never fully comprehend His ability to provide us with greatness beyond our measure. By trusting in Him no matter what the circumstance is, we can be victorious. When we take the ceiling off of God, stop limiting Him with our earthly thinking and give Him our whole trust; we must believe that He will always deliver on His promises. By walking the divine road of faith, all things are possible if asked in the name of Jesus Christ.

Proverbs 3:5 - Trust in the LORD with all thine heart; and lean not unto thine own understanding.

Hebrews 11:6 - But without faith [it is] impossible to please [him]: for he that cometh to God must believe that he is, and [that] he is a rewarder of them that diligently seek him.

Ephesians 2:8-9-For by grace are ye saved through faith; and that not of yourselves: [it is] the gift of God:

9 Not of works, lest any man should boast.

1 Peter 1:7 - That the trial of your faith, being much more precious than of gold that perisheth, though it be tried with fire, might be found unto praise and honour and glory at the appearing of Jesus Christ:

Isaiah 40:31 - But they that wait upon the LORD shall renew [their] strength; they shall mount up with wings as eagles; they shall run, and not be weary; [and] they shall walk, and not faint.

Hebrews 6:12 - That ye be not slothful, but followers of them who through faith and patience inherit the promises.

Hebrews 11:1- Now faith is the substance of things hoped for, the evidence of things not seen

NOTES:

RELEASE

Allow (something) to move, act, or flow freely

The action or process of releasing or being released.

Release, this has to be one of the hardest things for us to do. I don't mean forgiveness although sometimes they go hand in hand. I am referring to releasing the things in your life that you feel you need to control. For me, on day seven of my hospital stay, God revealed to me that there were many things that I had to release and give over to Him. He could do things that I could only hope for. Also, by giving things over to God, you release yourself of the burden. Therefore, God gets the praise and the glory when His work is done. For me one of the most difficult challenges, was to release my two children from my previous marriage. I experienced a terrible separation and divorce, and spent a lot of days over the next ten years doing everything in my power to protect them and keep them happy. I was the person that my children came to for everything. I convinced myself that it was my responsibility to solve all their problems and carry all their burdens. I figured God made me strong enough to do so. What I was missing was that God has His own plans for my children, and in order for them to build faith in Him they alone had to seek Him and not rely on me to fix it all. Yes, when your kids are small it is your responsibility to protect, nurture and pray for them. These things will never stop being a parent's job or responsibility. But there comes a time when you have to turn your children over and release them to seek God and walk the path that He has set for them. Also, they build a relationship with God that is intimate and personal. This was extremely hard for me because I had spent so much time raising my children and comforting them all their lives. I was following the belief that this is what a strong father was meant to do until I died. God said to me, on this day, that He loved my kids more than I did, so why was I harboring them from showing them how to build a life and relationship with Him? This revelation was life altering because it truly showed me how much God wants a relationship with my kids if I just get out of the way. So I did. Basically, what God wants from us is to release any and all things that belong to him, that He places in our care; children, spouses, finances, possessions, etc. He even says cast your cares upon Him and He will make your walk in life lighter.

I have seen people pray to keep a sick person here on earth, who may be tired of this life and is ready to join God in heaven. But instead of releasing them and letting them go, they spend countless hours and days praying for that person to stay, because they just could not bear the thought of losing a loved one. This is such a selfish act on the part of many. Why not ask the individual if they are ready to leave here? If they say yes, then pray with them and ask that they leave peacefully. I'm not talking about someone who is just giving up. That's not my point at all. I'm talking about people that we know who may be going through a final transition in life or who have reached an age where they feel their time has come. But because of how much we love them and cannot see life without them, we put aside what agreement they may have made with God and we continue to override what it is that they truly want. If we would just release them and continue to pray what it is they are agreeing for, then we are walking in the sight of God's will for that individual. I remember when I lost my grandmother on Christmas Eve twenty six years ago. She had stopped taking her medication for a heart condition. She was tired and ready to go and be with the Lord. She didn't tell anyone because she knew that everyone would be praying and begging her to reconsider. She was an awesome woman of God and this was her time. She knew that the family would not understand her decision and that the love that we all had for her would get in the way. To this day, some of us in the family still have not released her to God and continue to carry the burden of her absence. I questioned why she left this earth so early, but I also know that it would have been wrong of me to try and make her stay here for my sake. I was fourteen when she passed and I remember seeing her on the night of her passing and the radiant look she had. She was in Gods glory. She didn't look tired or stressed. She was beautiful and youthful as God had intended for her to be. What I saw that night was a woman of God who was in the presence of her Maker and I would never go against that no matter how painful the feeling of losing her would be.

Many of us have been raised to believe that whenever you are going through a tough time, whether it's with a job, children, spouse, or even health, that we search and find way of dealing with these issues on our own. Instead we stress, get frustrated, angry and even want to give up. This is not the life that

God has planned for any of us. He wants us to release all our worries and burdens to Him. He reassures us that when we do this, our life will be better. We will be more at peace and without the stress that we continually live with day in and day out. Pharmaceutical companies bank on the stressors in our lives with the hope that they can medicate our problems away. With God all you do is cast your problems on Him and He will deliver. Think about when you were a child (or if you've had small children.) Remember the comfort and security you had when a parent told you not to worry, that they will handle it? Or that when your small one has come to you, you reiterated the same thing that you heard as a child? The look they gave you knowing that they could rest in your words was always warming. Some people never had parents who said these words to them; or have children of their own to say these words to. But in either case whether it was another family member or a friend or co-worker hearing someone say that your problems will be handled and not to worry, is always reassuring. That's what God wants for us. He wants us to lay it all on Him and rest assured that our prayers will be answered. We must all go through challenges in order to have situations, (whether big or small obstacles), that we can give over to Him, so our faith in Him grows as well as living a less stressful life.

Psalms 55:22-Cast thy burden upon the LORD, and he shall sustain thee: he shall never suffer the righteous to be moved.

Isaiah 10:27-And it shall come to pass in that day, that his burden shall be taken away from off thy shoulder, and his yoke from off thy neck, and the yoke shall be destroyed because of the anointing.

Matthew 11:30-For my yoke is easy, and my burden is light

NOTES:

FORGIVENESS

The act of forgiving someone. The attitude of someone who is willing to forgive other people.

Forgiveness, a word of great volume. So many people say "I forgive you," myself included, but never really forgive. Jesus said while hanging on the cross, "Father forgive them for they know not what they do." This is epic. He was being crucified and even in His last moments, He asked that those who were committing such an evil act, be forgiven. How many of us would do that? Not many I'm sure. It goes to show how large Jesus' heart is. He continued to forgive out of the love that He has for mankind. On day eight of my hospital stay, this is the lesson that God wanted me to learn. If every time someone did something to hurt us, we forgave them the way Jesus forgave on that day, we would all be in a better place. We tend to hold on to the hurt that someone causes us and over time that hurt and anguish can build into something like sickness or even death. Someone will likely hurt us one way or another. Whether their actions were intentional or not, forgiving them is not for them as much as it is a way for you to clear yourself of the hurt and problems that attach themselves to you out of your lack of forgiveness. We probably know that mean or surly person that uses negativity in conversation or just looks at the world as a disappointment because of the things that people have done to them. What about the person whose body aches and is always complaining about physical ailments, but the doctors cannot find anything physically wrong with them? It is the lack of forgiveness. And walking around with this hatred for someone because they chose not to let go of what someone did to them. Lack of forgiving then becomes a burden. Not forgiving can eat you up and you will never be at peace. So many see forgiveness as a sign a weakness, "waving the white flag" so to speak. This could not be further from the truth. When someone does something against you with malice and you forgive them and release them to God, He will restore you of whatever it is that they tried to take from you. In turn they may end up seeking your forgiveness after God shows them the error of their ways. Leaving vengeance to God is the way we can continue to walk in peace. The devil will put things and people in our lives to test our ability to forgive, because he also knows that if we don't forgive others, how can we expect to be forgiven of our own iniquities? I'm not saying that once you forgive someone that everything is back to normal. It may take a long time to heal from the hurt that someone caused you, but by forgiving them you release yourself of carrying that burden that can ultimately destroy you. By forgiving someone you go from being a victim, to a conqueror. By not forgiving someone, you give them power over you. I know of forgiveness all too well. I ultimately have had to forgive people that I had previously grown to hate. I would take whatever they did to me and suppress it. And over time, I would explode or lash out at those that had nothing to do with my anger. I eventually would go days on end with headaches and body pain. This is how I lived for years. Until one day, about two weeks before my surgery, my mother told me to write down the names of all the people that had done something wrong to me in my past. Needless to say, the names took up about a full page. Now I had to ask God to forgive them and I also had to pray that God blessed them. I was taken aback. Why would I pray and forgive someone who purposely tried to do me harm whether it was physically or emotionally? Nevertheless, I was obedient and did what she asked.

It wasn't until I was in the hospital that I got the revelation as to why I did what I did. God said to me, "Forgive them for they know not what they do." This sounded utterly familiar. These are the words that Jesus cried out on the cross. Whatever anyone has done to me doesn't even come close to the pain and suffering that Jesus went through and even then He still has enough compassion in Him to ask His Father to forgive them. Talk about leading by example! I have since forgiven all those that have crossed me, but I even took it a step further. I also asked forgiveness of those who at some point I may have done something to that was hurtful. This way I free them, as well as myself, and I can focus on the blessing that God has for me. I no longer choose to carry the burden of unforgiveness. If God can forgive me then who am I to not forgive others?

Matthew 6:15 - But if ye forgive not men their trespasses, neither will your Father forgive your trespasses.

Luke 6:37 - Judge not, and ye shall not be judged: condemn not, and ye shall not be condemned: forgive, and ye shall be forgiven:

Ephesians 4:32 - And be ye kind one to another, tenderhearted, forgiving one another, even as God for Christ's sake hath forgiven you

NOTES:

WORDS

A sound or combination of sounds that has a meaning and is spoken or written

A brief remark or conversation: something that a person says

An order or command

It's been nine days since I first came into the hospital. Two surgeries down and an extensive road to recovery. This is when you can start to grow weary as I was at this very moment. Doctors coming into my room with the same questions, checking my stitches, listening to my heart and lungs and checking my surgery site to make sure the blood flow to my face was going well. Don't get me wrong, I am thankful that they took extreme care, but I wanted only one thing; to be home with my family and surround myself with them. My wife continued to come to see me and every day all I wanted to do was pack my belongings and walk out with her. I was learning how to walk with a cane, because part of my hip had to be removed to use as an artificial cheek bone below my right eye. It was during days like this that I had to reassure myself through prayer and also through words of encouragement. It was on this ninth day that God reminded me that the words that I speak would ultimately bless me or hinder my recovery. God gave us the gift of speech to say what it is that we want or don't want, what we're believing, or simply to express how we feel. When God created the world He didn't write it down or think it into existence. He simply spoke it and there it was. He spoke light out of darkness and created mankind by His words. In the Bible it says, that life and death are in the power of the tongue. The things that we want or are believing for, we must confess those things to be taken care of and most of all believe what we have spoken, as long as it is in line with Gods will for us. Every day that the doctors came in to see me and asked how I was doing. I would always reply, "better than yesterday and I will be even better tomorrow". I would confess this every day. I was standing on God's promise to me that my outcome was to be better than I could ever expect and by confessing it I was proving His promise to me. We can negate blessings and even bring upon certain illnesses just by speaking it. I was being shown on this day in the form of a spiritual vision, that when we speak, we give life to our words. In turn our words become a living thing that we set out into the world to either bless us and someone else or curse us. Take for example, you get a call that you are being promoted. You go into the interview and the person interviewing you is not very personable and makes you feel like they are not impressed. After the interview you walk out and immediately say that because they were not warm to you that you didn't get the job. By speaking that, you could negate what you may have been blessed with. Instead, your first thought should be that although they weren't receptive to you, God can intervene and if it's His will, you will succeed in getting the promotion and by trusting God and believing, you set yourself up for Him to bless you. The same goes for when we become ill or diagnosed with a deadly disease. When I was diagnosed with cancer, what I said after they told me was to be the life or death of my existence. It was hard to hear and looking at my wife crying, I had to stand on the belief that God had bigger plans for me and this was not the end. I immediately said while the doctor was in the room, that I would be cured of this and I would live my life cancer free. I had been through a tough, troubled life and now I was blessed with a wonderful wife and family. I believed that God would not bless me with these wonderful gifts only to leave them. I knew this to be certain. Now it was up to me to stand on His word and trust and pray for a long life without cancer. I never heard of a high grade sarcoma. It had grown to three millimeters in a month. It was aggressive. Now everything was on the table. After leaving the hospital, my wife and I agreed in the car that this would not be the end of my life. We boldly prayed to God and asked Him to work miracles to remove this tumor; not to return me to my old self, but to renew me and us in Him. After my diagnosis, before we went into every doctor's appointment, we prayed and spoke what we were believing for. And that was whoever was to perform my surgery, that it would be done with excellence, and it would be the best surgery that they had done to date. After my surgeries, every doctor that came to see me specifically said, that I was a challenge, but my outcome was the best surgery they had ever performed. This is what God said would happen and this is what we spoke every day. It really doesn't matter what you're going through in life, what you speak can change it for the good or for the worse. We all have a choice to use our words to enhance our life or to destroy our life. Speak success, prosperity, health and happiness into your life. I'm not saying that things will not come up to challenge you in many different situations, but your first line of defense, is to speak against it and believe that the words that you released out of your mouth will land on God's ears and He will make it right according to His will. This is what He wants from us. Negative thoughts become negative words, which in turn can become a negative outcome. You can't expect longevity and prosperity, if you continually speak negativity into your life.

Proverbs 18:21-Death and life are in the power of the tongue: and they that love it shall eat the fruit thereof

Psalms 35:28-And my tongue shall speak of thy righteousness and of thy praise all the day long.

Job 6:24-Teach me, and I will hold my tongue: and cause me to understand wherein I have erred.

John 12:50- And I know that his commandment is life everlasting: whatsoever I speak therefore, even as the Father said unto me, so I speak.

NOTES:

PRAYER

A solemn request for help or expression of thanks addressed to God or an object of worship.

An earnest hope or wish

When it comes to prayer, I wasn't well versed. I later found out that prayer is the major highway of communication between you and God. Prayer is the way to show God, that you are coming to Him the way a child comes to his father, to repair or solve a problem. It's a conversation. I always thought that prayer had to be direct and formal, until I had the opportunity to hear from God on the tenth day of my hospitalization. Sometimes prayer is so simple that we overlook it. It's as if you are having a conversation with a family member or friend. God wants this open line, because it shows Him how much we trust Him and the direction that He may send us. Growing up, I always thought that prayer had to be this big thing that only those closest to God could perform. It wasn't until I was diagnosed with cancer, that I got the chance to just speak to God and tell Him my worries and concerns; turning over what I could not change myself, to Him. I always saw my parents pray, but they would be so consumed by their praying and speaking in tongues, that I felt that it would take ages for me to be able to speak with God with the same intensity that they did. God, on the other hand just wanted me to talk to Him and give all my concerns over to Him. Once diagnosed I figured "Hey, what do I have to lose"? My family and I prayed that God would work miracles when it came to my surgery and treatment. God answered by saying that my surgery and healing would be better than could be expected. Now with that being said, who am I to question God? If He said not to worry, then why worry? I gave it over to Him and every day since my diagnosis I have given every circumstance over to Him, whether good or bad. God wants us to ask Him what's next, so He can guide us to the next step in our lives. Just like a parent does with their children. If we don't ask God for anything, then how can we expect Him to deliver on everything? I have learned that even though man may not make good on his promises to you, God in His time, will always deliver. He said that my surgery would be better than expected and it was. They removed all the cancerous tissue from my face and even though I will be left with scarring, that is nothing in comparison to being cancer free. I will, from this moment forward, trust God to deliver on His promises to me and thank Him for what He has already done.

Psalms 4:1-(To the chief Musician on Neginoth, A Psalm of David.) Hear me when I call, O God of my righteousness: thou hast enlarged me when I was in distress; have mercy upon me, and hear my prayer

Psalms 5:3-My voice shalt thou hear in the morning, O LORD; in the morning will I direct my prayer unto thee, and will look up

Matthew 21:22-And all things, whatsoever ye shall ask in prayer, believing, ye shall receive

NOTES:

GODS WORD (THE BIBLE)

The Bible, what exactly is it? For the longest time, I thought the Bible was just something that was always around the house, that my mother or grandmother would recite from during a rough time or for prayer. The Bible to me didn't really have much value. It was just a book that collected dust and was put where all other books go, on the bookcase or maybe the end table. It wasn't until my eleventh day in the hospital, that I found what the Bible really was....It was the voice of God and His thoughts written through the hands of men. The Bible is actually God's thought process and it's His instruction manual for our daily lives. Everything that we need to survive is written in these old scribes as they were inspired by God. God gave us scriptures to recite, when we are in need and also for when we just want to be thankful. I remember some time ago, I would not stay in a hotel unless there was a Bible in the drawer next to my bed. It gave me a sense of peace even though I didn't, at that time, understand the full magnitude of this magnificent book. I was always compelled to read the Bible and it wasn't until I was laying in the hospital that I was able to see the true reason why it was given to us. It was given to us to live by, to guide us, and give us the knowledge we need to get closer to what God has designed for us in this lifetime. It is God's actual spoken words. This alone blew me away. Just knowing the Creator of heaven and earth, has taken the time to actually let us get a glimpse of how mighty He is, by giving us insight to how He thinks. Here is the most astonishing part....God is the Word. It is written in the Bible that God said, "That in the beginning there was the Word". He was referring to Himself. The Word (God) has always been here. He is the beginning and the end of time. God's words, the actual words that we read in the Bible transcend through time. God is the Word and God is always present, past and future. Yes, in the Bible it speaks of disciples, people long ago, kings and pharaohs, among others. But there is a message in all of these parables and stories and it leads ultimately back to the word that was spoken by God Himself. I have always believed that when someone writes a letter to you, it's very intimate. It's a personal insight as to that person's deepest thoughts. We live in a world of emails, texting and video chats, but to me, reading a hand written letter is so much more. The Bible is God's hand written letter to all of us. It's His intimate thoughts. It is Him showing how much He loves us, by giving us the tool that we need to be with Him eternally. The Bible is so much more than just a book, it's our way of life.

John 1:1-In the beginning was the Word, and the Word was with God, and the Word was God

John 1:14-And the Word was made flesh, and dwelt among us, (and we beheld his glory, the glory as of the only begotten of the Father,) full of grace and truth

Acts 6:4-But we will give ourselves continually to prayer, and to the ministry of the word

Revelation 19:13: And he was clothed with a vesture dipped in blood: and his name is called The Word of God

NOTES:

REFLECTION

Morning of release day

Serious thought or consideration.

It is 1 a.m. on the twelfth day since I first walked into this hospital and I will be leaving a different man, anyway you look at it. Not just my physical appearance, but also my spirit and soul will be changed forever. I feel blessed that God took this time to show me all that He has shown me. He has opened my eyes to what it is like to live a life with Him that does not have to be what I was so accustomed to. As I look out my window, I ask God to reveal to me, a glimpse of where He has brought me from and that I have so much to be thankful for. As I fall back into my chair and put my feet up on my hospital bed, my little girl and my wife immediately pop into my head. After that, I see the faces of my two older children, then my brother, his wife and my niece and nephew. Right beside them, are my parents. I continue to see other faces in my thoughts of people that God has used along my journey; my oncologist and my surgeons. The odd thing is, that at the end of the face scrolling I see my face. Not the after surgery or even pre-surgery face for that matter, but I see a renewed me staring right back at me as if I was in the room with myself. I asked God, "Why are you showing me myself?" God answered, "This is the new you, restored." I can honestly admit, that I didn't recognize this new me, for there were no scars or looks of scorn on my face, just a look of peace and love. Something that in my forty years of being on this earth, I can honestly say I didn't see much of. What God did in me, was a complete transformation. As I continued to sit in my chair, I once again felt an enormous amount of peace come over me, as if I was being engulfed. I asked God "Why was it me that You chose to pour your love onto?" His simple reply was, "Why not you?" His words were so comforting. I knew that when I left the hospital, that's when the real healing was to happen. I was actually feeling down, because I was enjoying so much of God's time and I knew that when I went home, life was waiting for me. I was scared to go back to the old me, with all the stress, headaches and sleepless nights. But, I was also eager to see my family and love on them, because I had a new-found love for them. Even though I would not be in the ambience of God's presence all the time, He said that He would never leave us nor forsake us. I would rest assured in these words, after I left the hospital and continued my healing at home.

Reflecting really was just about me taking time to actually accept and own the fact that I had cancer. Once my biopsy came back positive, I immediately went into survival mode. All I could think about was how to survive the diagnosis and what it would do to my family if I didn't. As I was looking around my room, I was actually thinking "Man you came in with cancer and now you're leaving without it." You don't really have time to think about anything other than survival when you are diagnosed. It's not until those late nights or early mornings like this one, when you are actually faced with it. I don't know why or how I got it, but it doesn't matter now. Actually it never mattered how or why. Just the need to stay alive is all that was important.

RELEASE DAY
Continued

I am scheduled to leave the hospital by 10 a.m. My wife is on her way and so is my brother. I have been up since 5 a.m., packing and preparing to go. I decided to take one last look around at the place where God and I had spent so many hours together. He has completely renewed me and even though I still had a long way to go, I would not be going alone. He would be beside me and ahead of me, guiding me with His love and mercy. The doctors came in for the last time to check on me. Since the beginning surgery, to the last day, they were in awe with how well my procedure went and how rapidly I was recovering. This was one of the most difficult surgeries that they have ever done. I truly believe that if it wasn't for the prayers and my faith in God and trusting Him and His word, that all things are possible through Him, that I would have had a different outcome. Once my brother and my wife got to the hospital, I was waiting. I was all packed and all they had to do was wheel me downstairs and out the door. Although I could not wait to get out into the fresh air, I also felt like a child leaving the comforting hold of a parent. I was safe in the hospital. I didn't want to lose the comfort of God's hands on me. I had never felt such a connection to God as I had being in the hospital and I didn't want it to end. In all it was bitter sweet. I was wheeled down by my brother to the front of the hospital while we waited for the valet to bring the truck. It was noisy and actually raining. I had spent twelve days with God and I could never go back to where or who I was before the hand of God rested on me. And for the twelve days where He blessed me with his presence, I will spend every day of the rest of my life following Him.

CONCLUSION

Cancer in itself, is a scary disease. So many people perish from it every day. I never in a million years thought that I would be diagnosed with any kind of disease, especially cancer. It was a devastating blow to me and my family. I can say this, with all my mind, body, and soul, that if I did not seek God and through the prayers of so many, I would not be here today. God honestly showed me in the hospital how much love He has not just for me, but for all who believe and follow Him and His Son Jesus. He has given me a new lease on life and with this new chance, I have an obligation to share this story with anyone who chooses to read it. I hope that any person who may be going through any kind of life altering situation, will find the reverence and peace that I found, during my "Twelve Days" in the hospital. God is real and He is alive. His Son Jesus is seated right beside Him, waiting for us to call out to Him and ask for His forgiveness, help and guidance. He wants to bring us closer to Him and sometimes through the hardest times, we can find the strength to continue, if we give it over to God and let Him carry us through. I will never see my life the same way I did prior to getting cancer, but I am so thankful that I was able to walk with God during this time and ultimately change my life forever.

Printed in Great Britain
by Amazon